For our
dear Lena and Remo,
who, despite so many
emotions and events,
are two wonderful,
cheerful and carefree
children.

DinoLena

The brave little girl that teaches the small Langerhans cells how to swim.

© 2022 Translation: Paula Ruckstuhl
ISBN 978-3-9525656-3-6 (Hardcover)
ISBN 978-3-9525656-7-4 (eBook)
ISBN 978-3-9525656-9-8 (Paperback)

Original title:

DinoLena - Het dappere meisje dat de Langerhanscelletjes zwemmen leert.
© 2022 Paula Ruckstuhl
ISBN 978-3-9525656-0-5 (Hardcover)
ISBN 978-3-9525656-4-3 (eBook)
ISBN 978-3-9525656-8-1 (Paperback)

Also available as:

• DinoLena - S'tapfere Meitli, wo dä chline Langerhans-Zelle schwümme biibringt.
  (Schweizerdeutsch)
• DinoLena - Das tapfere Mädchen, das den kleinen Langerhans-Zellen das Schwimmen
  beibringt (Deutsch)
DinoLena is published by Paula Ruckstuhl

© Idea and Text 2022: Paula Ruckstuhl
© Illustrations 2022: Roosmarijn Nagel
© Creative Design: Linda Retel

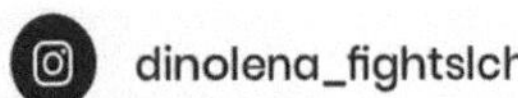
dinolena_fightsIch

dinolena.fightsIch@gmail.com

How it started...

This is Lena. She is also known as DinoLena, because she is strong like a dinosaur. Can you see her muscles?

Lena has a twin brother; his name is Remo. They also call him SuperRemo, since he is the best brother you can have, and he is always there for Lena. Together with their mum and dad they undertake all kinds of adventures.

When Lena was only 2 years old,
she suddenly got very thirsty.
Wherever there was water, she
immediately took a sip. Once,
after it had rained heavily, she
even emptied the water that
had collected in the trailer of
the Bobbycar into her mouth.

The doctor said that she shouldn't drink so much, but it was very difficult for her. She also had to wee all the time and therefore needed so much water. She got angry and also very sad. Then she went to the hospital with her mummy. After a very long night, the doctor knew why Lena was always so thirsty.

First Lena got
a magic spray

When she takes this, she is suddenly no longer thirsty
and can do what every child should do...

...play to her heart's content and above all,
enjoy herself!

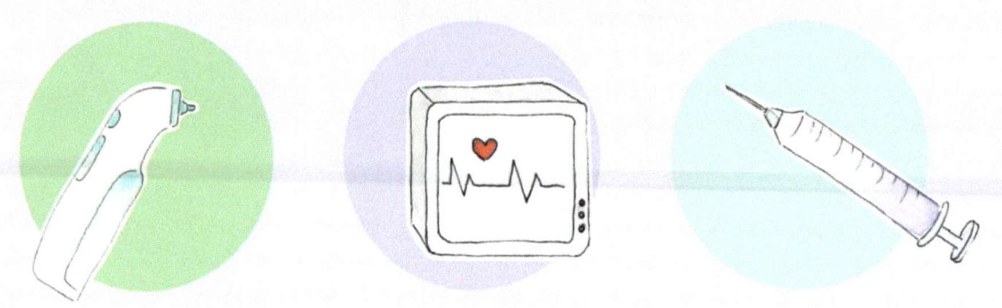

To find out why Lena suddenly needs
a magic spray and other children don't,
Lena had to have special tests in the hospital.

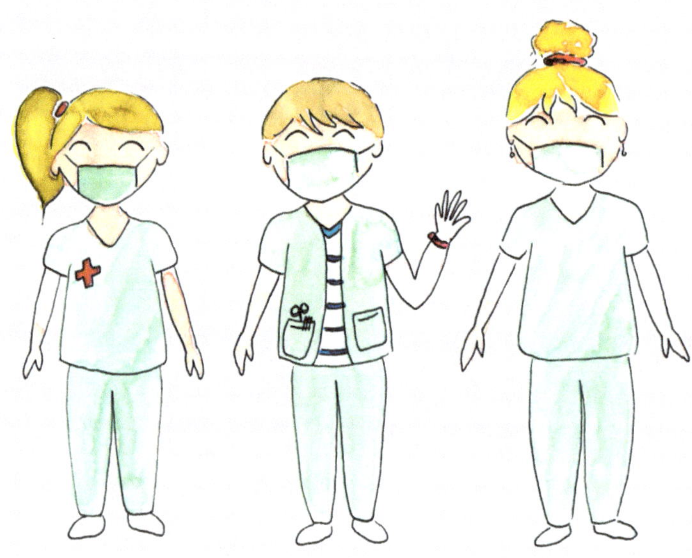

In the hospital there were green people everywhere. These are doctors and nurses. They carefully examined Lena. Pictures were taken of Lena's tummy and head, and they even made a small video of her heart. Luckily, the doctors gave her something to sleep while she was examined.

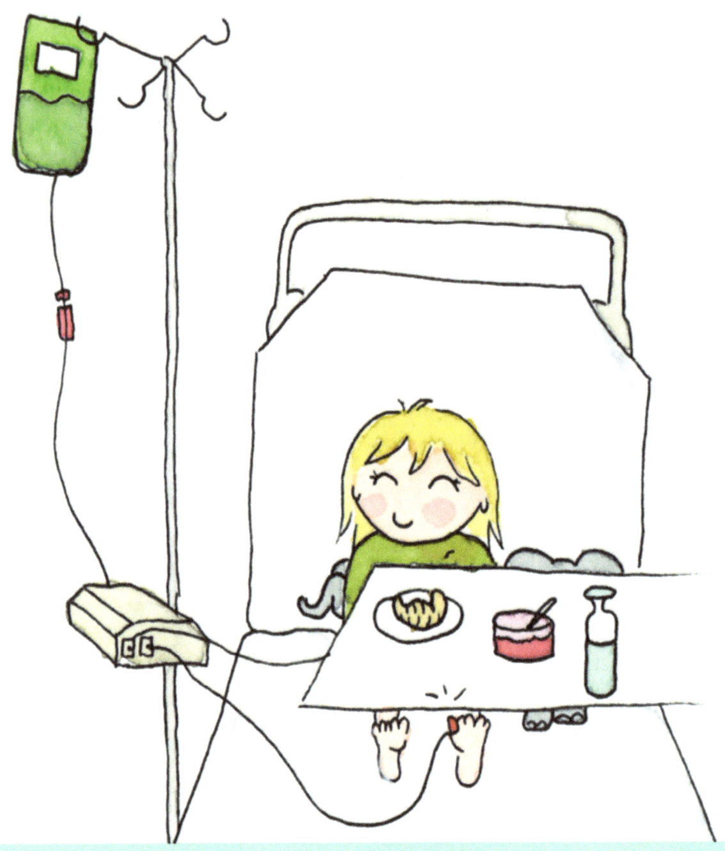

When she woke up, she could eat all she wanted. Her favourite foods were Birchermüsli, grapes and croissants. Oh how delicious! Then she would call herself a really lucky girl.

Finally
the doctors knew
what was going
on with Lena...

The Small Langerhans Cells...

All people, even grown-ups, have all kinds of cells in their bodies. They swim there, to make sure you will grow and stay healthy.

In some of the grown-ups and kids however, there are also many small baby cells that cannot swim at all! Together they will look for a place to hold on to. You can find them in all different places, in your leg, mouth, tummy and even on your skin.

With Lena the
place where
the baby cells
are holding
themselves tight
is in her head.

Having all these little baby cells in a heap is obviously not so handy, because then other cells can no longer do what they have to do. This could mean for example, that you suddenly have to wee a lot and get very, very thirsty. It is therefore very, very important that the baby cells learn to swim!

Fortunately,
there are very
special little helpers
who are happy
to help Lena...

Can you
keep a little
secret?
A little
magic door

After the examinations, a tiny magic door was placed in Lena's chest. Through this door the little helpers come in to teach Lena's baby cells how to swim!

To open the secret little door, Lena goes back to the hospital every week. She then brings her own doctor's case and helps her own team of doctors who all support her to be such a brave and strong little girl! There are also many sweet and funny clowns, one of them is called professor Flippa and she is the smartest of all!

First DinoLena has to show her finger, a small sting follows and then a tiny red train pulls out. It feels a little weird, but luckily that passes quickly.

Afterwards she is allowed to climb onto the bed and is examined by the doctor. There is even a TV in the room, since the long wait is sometimes very boring.

Now Lena can show her magic little door.
At home, mummy has already put a magic
plaster on it so that it can be opened easily.

First the entrance has to be cleaned very well. For that, the penguins arrive and shuffle around with their little feet. The feet smell a bit funny and are also very cold because they obviously have been standing in the snow. Brrrr!

And then.... the magic door is opened briefly to let the little helpers in. The grown-ups also call that chemotherapy, but that is not such a nice word.

Sometimes the doctor lets something slide out of the little door, namely a red train! Sometimes even more than one. Lena chooses where the journey should go and helps the people get off at the train station. She can rotate the train 10 times, **are you counting?** 1..2..3..4..5..6..7..8..9..10! Then the trains are taken to the laboratory to see if DinoLena is still as strong as usual.

DiN

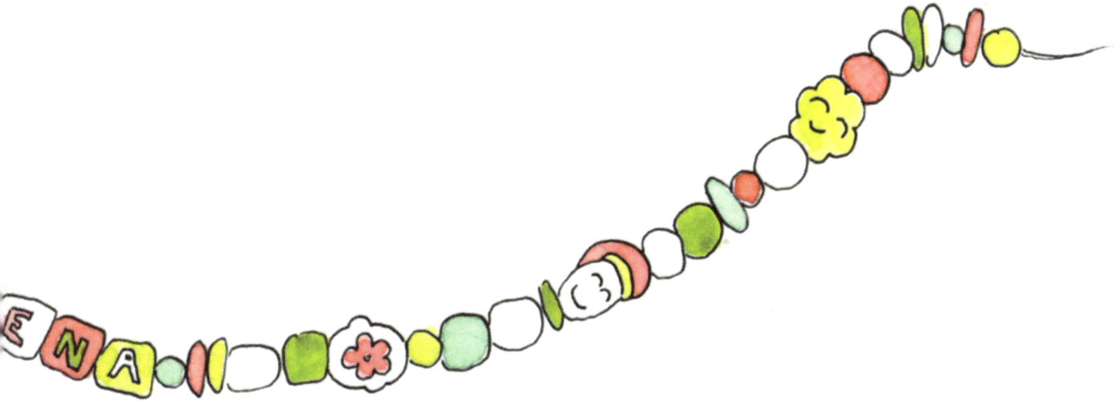

When all the little helpers are inside, the doctor lets in a bit of 'spaghetti water' so that the little helpers can start their swimming class and the door can be closed again. For being such a great and brave little helper herself, Lena can choose 4 pearls for her own DinoLena chain.

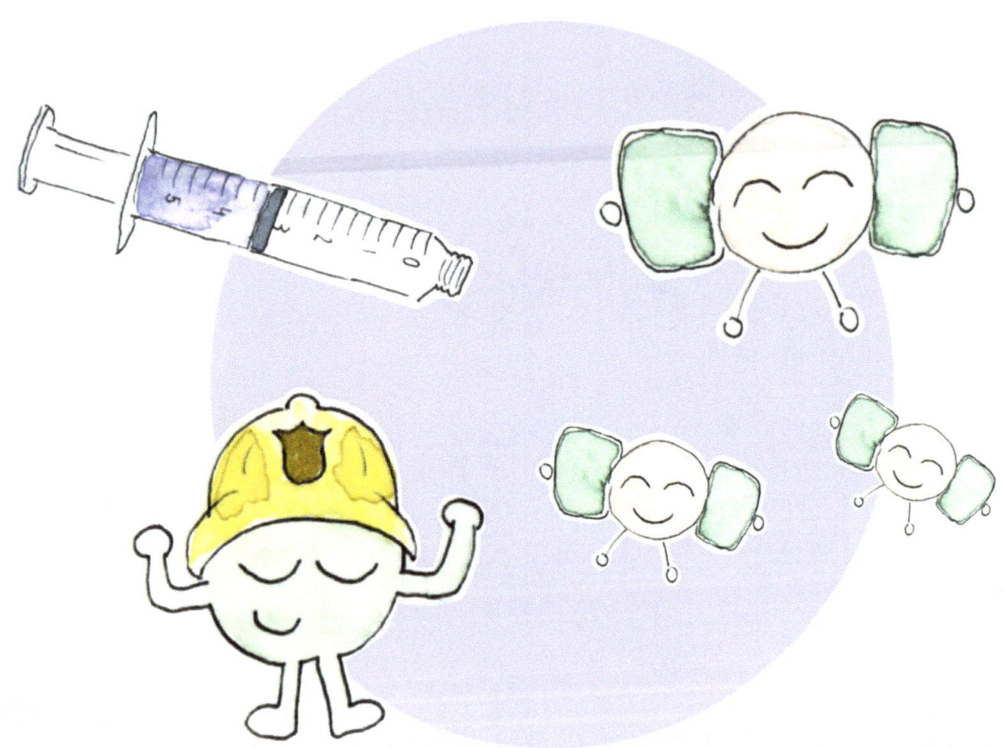

When Lena is at home, she takes syrup shots daily to make the little helpers stronger, they also have to eat of course! From time-to-time Lena drives back to the hospital to have pictures taken to see if the baby cells have already learned how to swim a bit. Until then, brave little DinoLena helps the little helpers through her magic door!

For the grown-ups...

When Lena was 2 years old, she suddenly started drinking a lot. It was thought to be psychological, and we were advised not to let her drink more than 2 liters of water a day. This was extremely difficult, and her behaviour changed. A happy child turned into a sad and sometimes even aggressive girl. She only wanted water-rich food like cucumber and tomato and her skin dried out. She really did everything to get water. As soon as she got water she felt better immediately, only problem was that this equated to 4 to 6 liters per day. After many visits to the doctor and persistence from our side, an intense water deprivation test was carried out and she got the diagnosis of Diabetes Insipidus Centralis or 'Water Diabetes'.

This condition prevents the pituitary gland from producing the 'water' hormone ADH. As a result, the body is unable to retain water. To compensate for the loss of fluids, you must drink a lot. Fortunately, this hormone is available as a medicine, which stabilizes the fluid balance and can improve the quality of life.

An MRI was performed to rule out that the cause was other than congenital. This led to the next diagnosis, namely Langerhans Cell Histiocytosis (LCH). This is a very rare disease.

Certain white blood cells – the Langerhans cells – multiply at an unusual rate and form tumors that can deposit in the bones, sometimes also in various organs or in the brain. As a result, the function of the affected body part may be compromised. The consequences can often be treated, but it is a long and difficult path. Unfortunately, there is also no guarantee that the disease will not reappear elsewhere in the body.

With Lena, the tumors are in the head: in the cranial bone and in the pituitary gland. In order to be able to combat the consequences, the cause – i.e. the tumors – must be treated. At present Lena is in the middle of treatment with chemotherapy and cortisone, to which she is fortunately responding very well.

We always try to stay positive. This helps Lena to approach and endure the treatments without fear. The team at the Zurich Children's Hospital also plays a very important role for us there. They include Lena in a lot of what they do, she likes to help and is allowed to do so. But since she is still so small, it is difficult for us to explain to her and her brother why she always has to go to the hospital and take medication that sometimes makes her feel bad. From the beginning we made up little stories during the hospital visits to make the different situations easier to understand.

That is where the idea for this little book came from. We hope that other children and their families who have to experience something similar can also benefit from the story of DinoLena.

The 'Langerhans Cell Histiocytosis Awareness' Facebook group, where affected people from all over the world can share their stories and experiences, has given us a lot of strength and support as parents. Super Sebbie's booklet, about a boy affected by LCH, the websites Histio.org and Histiozytose.org also contain a lot of information and enable interactive exchange.

We hope that you find Lenas's story helpful and that you above all enjoy the book!